Whatever. I'm going to nail this competition!

Sharks vs. Sloths

★ Julie Beer ★

NATIONAL GEOGRAPHIC KiDS

BROWN-THROATED SLOTH

Washington, D.C.

Contents

GO SLOTH!

GO Shark!

SPORTS

Hey there, loyal fans! We're back at Animal Showdown Stadium for a competition unlike any we've seen before!

Isn't that the truth, Bob! We should call this the battle of outrageous opposites: Land versus sea. Slow versus fast. Furry versus sleek. I wonder if there's anything these two competitors have in common?

I can think of something, Peggy—awesomeness!

Haha! You got me there, Bob. These have got to be two of the coolest creatures on the planet! But I've got to warn you: I have a sneaking suspicion we're in for a few surprises. Spoiler alert! Being slow doesn't mean you can't sometimes win the race. And as far as tough guys go, sometimes they have an unexpected softer side.

Well, if that isn't a teaser, I don't know what is! It looks like we're going to need some help to see which of these opposites is going to attract the winner's trophy. Think the kid holding this book is up for the job?

Absolutely! Thanks, kid! Now that we have our judge, let's get this show on the road and introduce the contenders!

You got it! Swinging in ever so slowly from this corner is a fella who loves hanging around upside down. Don't let that wide, goofy grin fool you: He has plenty of tricks up his shaggy sleeves. Let's hear your loudest shout for the one and only Sloth!

And making a splash in this corner is a gal who's ready to sink her teeth into this competition. She's big, she's powerful ... why, she's one of the top predators of the sea. Put your fins together for Shark!

Wow! Adorable and huggable versus fierce and legendary? Well isn't that a different kettle of fish! I'm going to need a refresher on how we determine our winner.

It's pretty simple. We're going to present 22 categories—from Biggest Appetite to Weirdest Quirk to Best Smile. But our reader friend here is going to make the final call and decide who's the winner.

I can't wait to see what they decide! Let's get this throwdown started!

Hey, Kid! Time for a shout-out!

GO SLOTH! HANG IN THERE!

GO SHARK! YOU'RE JAWSOME!

Meet the Contenders

Before we put the gloves on, let's pause and greet our competitors.

SLOTHS

Straight from the tropical forests of Central and South America is a creature who permanently lives life in the slow lane. You may have heard of two-toed and three-toed sloths, but did you know that within those groupings there are six different species? They all share an easygoing vibe, but don't be quick to slap the couch potato label on these tree dwellers. It's true, they're chill, but prepare to be amazed at some of their groovy skills.

Maned (three-toed)

Three-toed

Brown-throated

Pale-throated

Pygmy

Two-toed

Hoffman's

Linnaeus's

FYI: Three-toed sloths have one more claw on their forelimb than two-toed sloths have

SHARKS

You can't dip a toe in any of Earth's oceans and not share the water with a shark. Sharks. Are. Everywhere. But erase that image in your head of jagged triangular teeth and fins chasing after surfers. This is a sampling of 10 supercool sharks we feature in this book, but there are more than 400 species swimming in Earth's oceans, some shorter than a pencil! Sharks may play villains on-screen, but in real life, most shark species are like any other fish—just going with the flow.

Basking

Dwarf lantern

Gray reef

Greenland

Hammerhead

Mako

Nurse

Tiger

Whale

Great white

Look out for more species of sharks featured in this book!

Wait just one minute—400 species of sharks versus a mere six for sloths?

Are you wondering, "Where's the red flag warning?" Make like a sloth and chillax, folks. Have we learned nothing from *The Tortoise and the Hare*? This isn't a one-round battle. There could be some rough waters ahead for Shark. And there may be a moment when Sloth is clinging to a battle by just one toe. What this all comes down to is who YOU think is going to win this epic matchup! Are you going to hang in there and vote for Team Sloth? Or are you going to dive in headfirst and vote for Team Shark? Hold that thought! Why not wait a bit and weigh your options? There's plenty more to learn about these two competitors. Let the battle begin!

Battle of the Speediest

Okay, we might as well just get it over with and talk about the elephant in the room: Sloths are known as major slowpokes! Crack open a dictionary to the word "sloth" and right after "slow-moving mammal of tropical forests" you'll find another definition of the word: "lazy." Ouch! You're not exactly coming out of your corner swinging in this round, Sloth. But maybe there's a story behind Sloth's slo-mo ways. And what about Shark? Can we just assume she's going to win this battle on reputation alone? Let's find out!

Time-out for a fast fact:
GREENLAND SHARKS—THE SLOWEST-MOVING SHARKS—TAKE AFTER SLOTHS! THEY CRUISE AT LESS THAN A MILE AN HOUR (1.6 KM/H)— MUCH SLOWER THAN YOUR WALKING PACE.

BROWN-THROATED SLOTH

Sloths

Sloths are the slowest-moving mammal on Earth. When they're on the move, they cruise at a rate of six to eight feet (1.8 to 2.4 m) per minute. On an average day, they travel less than half the length of a football field! But in fairness, they have a good reason for their lack of speed: A low-cal leaf diet and slow digestion mean sloths need to conserve the little energy they have. Hanging out in treetops with their food source all around lets them do that. When they're on the ground, the tempo slows even more: Sloths can't walk. They get around by dragging themselves with their claws. Sloth may not be speedy, but he's got determination!

Looks like this mako has a taste for fast food!

Sharks

Passing on your left, Sloth! Shortfin makos—the world's fastest sharks—can speed through water at 35 miles an hour (56 km/h)! How do they do it? Makos have a unique, powerful tail stroke; their muscles are made to quickly take in oxygen, which lets them recover faster than other shark species; their head is shaped like a torpedo to efficiently move through water; and their tail is shaped like a crescent, allowing for less resistance. Why the hurry? Makos have to keep up with their lunch: tuna! Unfortunately for the Atlantic bluefin tuna, makos can outswim them by about 10 miles an hour (16 km/h).

MAKO SHARK

Battle of the Biggest

Do we even need to bring a measuring tape to this matchup?

Aren't sharks ginormous? After all, the longest ones, whale sharks, reach up to 55 feet (17 m) and can weigh more than 20 tons (18 t). Talk about blowing the sloths out of the water in this competition! But maybe we better back it up for a moment: Let's remember there are hundreds of species of sharks. One of the smallest, pygmy sharks, are a mere 10 inches (25 cm) long. That's the length of just three aquarium-size goldfish! Uh oh, Shark. You may be a fish out of water in this battle!

Now that we cleared the air on the awkward topic of speed, it's time to really size up the competition. Out in the wild, sloths and sharks don't ever have a chance to put their heads together to figure out who's bigger—the whole tropical forest versus sea thing sort of stands in the way. So it's high time we settle the score here. Based solely on size, which of these creatures can claim the title of biggest?

Time-out for a fast fact:
EACH WHALE SHARK HAS A UNIQUE PATTERN OF SPOTS AND STRIPES. NO TWO WHALE SHARKS LOOK EXACTLY ALIKE!

WHALE SHARK

Sloths

While sharks come in all shapes and sizes, sloths keep it pretty simple. There are two types of sloths: two-toed and three-toed. Now get ready to have your mind blown: Both two-toed and three-toed sloths have three toes! It turns out they get their name from the number of claws they have on their forelimbs (front legs), not the number on their hind limbs (back legs). (Three-fingered and two-fingered would make a lot more sense!) Adult two-toed sloths are about two feet (0.6 m) long and weigh about 17 pounds (7.7 kg). Three-toed sloths are slightly smaller. Both types are about the weight of a pug—which is way bigger than three goldfish. Depending on the shark species that Sloth is in the ring with, this battle still has a chance of being a fair fight!

BROWN-THROATED SLOTH

Weirdest Relatives

This competition is just getting started, but it's already clear that there isn't anything ordinary about either of these two competitors. But they've got nothing on their relatives from yesteryear! Let's find out who has the wackiest family tree.

Sharks

Sharks have been swimming in Earth's seas for 450 million years. That's before our planet even had trees! One of Shark's most impressive (and fearsome!) early relatives was megalodon, the biggest shark that ever lived. Cruising through the ocean as recently as 2.6 million years ago, the megalodon was up to 60 feet (18 m) long and had the strongest bite of any animal ever—powerful enough to crush a small car! It likely went extinct because of cooling ocean waters, and perhaps from rising competitors, like orcas (aka killer whales), who had the advantage of hunting in groups. Megalodon—which means "megatooth" because of its seven-inch (18-cm)-long teeth—caught his meals solo.

Sloths

Sloth's extinct relative, the giant ground sloth, may not have had the bite that Shark's relatives did, but it was mega in its own right. Megatheriidae, or "giant beast," didn't dangle from trees like modern sloths do, perhaps because it was as tall as an elephant. Its claws were more than 1.5 feet (46 cm) long— that's the length of two dinner knives lined up end to end! Originally living in South America about 60 million years ago, giant ground sloths eventually spread to North America, where they lived until about 4,200 years ago. These bygone sloths didn't just munch on leaves—they also ate avocados! Researchers believe giant ground sloths are partly to thank for spreading avocado seeds throughout the Americas (by pooping them after they ate them).

Time-out for a fast fact: SLOTHS' CLOSEST LIVING RELATIVES ARE ARMADILLOS AND ANTEATERS!

Thanks for the guac, Sloth!

Coolest Hangout

Sloth and Shark are clearly opposites, and the place they call home is no exception. Both have pretty sweet digs—wide-open waters with coral and the occasional sunken ship versus a warm tropical jungle with the sounds of wildlife buzzing all around. This throwdown is so evenly matched it may just be a matter of which you prefer: sea or trees?

Sloths

Who wouldn't want to live in a tree fort? Sloths have it made in the shade, calling the forests of Central and South America home. They spend almost all of their time in the tree canopy, each with a territory that covers the size of about 12 football fields. Sloths sometimes cross paths (and branches) with each other, but most of the time they're happy to chill solo. Pygmy three-toed sloths—the smallest species of three-toed sloth—are found only on one isolated island off the coast of Panama. And get this: When pygmy sloths get crust in their eyes—Hey, don't judge, a sloth likes to nap!—it's often red, from the pigment in the red mangrove leaves they eat!

Talk about being one with your habitat, Sloth!

HOFFMAN'S TWO-TOED SLOTHS

Sharks

Shark sure knows how to make herself at home.
Various species of sharks can be found in every single ocean on Earth. That's not to say that individual species don't have their own unique habitat. Take the frilled shark: This five-foot (1.5-m)-long eel-like shark with 300 teeth only lives in deep, dark waters in the Atlantic and Pacific Oceans. Then there are gray reef sharks: They cruise around the warm, shallow waters of coral atolls and lagoons next to reef habitats—specifically, in the Indian and Pacific Oceans. What's so special about this home turf? The sharks often hunt as a group—working together to trap fish next to the reef for a quick and easy snack.

GRAY REEF SHARKS

Biggest Appetite

If Sloth and Shark were to join each other for a meal, they most certainly wouldn't split an entrée. They don't exactly have the same taste. Sloths are some of the pickiest eaters you'll ever meet. And sharks, well, let's just say they've been known to literally eat junk as food!

Sloths

Both two-toed and three-toed sloths mostly eat leaves for breakfast ... and for lunch ... and for dinner. Hey, when you know what you like, why mix it up? They eat the leaves of a wide variety of trees, but the leaves have a low calorie count. Just like cows, sloths have a four-chambered stomach, and in pure sloth form, they are slow at digesting. Some animals that eat low-calorie foods eat massive quantities to bulk up. Not sloths. They are petite picky eaters who instead move less to conserve all the energy they have stored. And they rarely wash down all those leaves with water—they get almost all their water from the plants they eat.

Time-out for a fast fact: THREE-TOED SLOTHS ONLY EAT THE TYPES OF LEAVES THEIR MOM FED THEM WHEN THEY WERE BABIES.

HOFFMAN'S TWO-TOED SLOTH

Sharks

Depending on the species, sharks eat everything from fish to crustaceans to marine mammals—and even other sharks. The basking shark, the world's second largest shark, is massive—up to 46 feet (14 m) long—but its main food source, plankton, is itty-bitty—a mere 0.04 inch (1 mm) long. And then there are tiger sharks: the trash cans of the sea. They have been known to eat license plates, tires, paint cans, and video cameras! It's not that tiger sharks have a taste for junk; they are likely lured by the reflective metal, which could look like the shiny scales of a fish underwater, or they mistake trash for prey.

BASKING SHARK

Most Athletic

Wow, this matchup is looking pretty even! It's time to put a little muscle into the competition to tip the scales. Better roll up your sleeves, Sloth and Shark. It's time to find out who's the MVP!

Sharks

Shark has already proven that she's an all-star when it comes to speed in the water, but just wait until you hear what she can do in the air. Great white sharks like surprise attacks, so they position themselves underneath their prey—seals are a favorite—then speed upward for the munch. Great whites in South Africa have been seen leaping from the water—like a breaching whale—and then falling back with food in their mouth. Those acrobatic moves are thanks in part to the fact that sharks' skeletons are made of flexible tissue called cartilage—they don't have any bones!

GREAT WHITE SHARK

Sloths

Sloth might not look like he'd be on the varsity team, but don't go calling him a benchwarmer! We know that sloths aren't speedy, but here's a game changer: Sloths can swim! Occasionally dropping from their treetop perch to plop in a river below, sloths do the dog paddle to get around, and they move three times faster in the water than they do on land. Although Sloth has flexed some muscle in this category, big muscles aren't his strong suit. In order to save energy, sloths have very low muscle mass. They may look round, and even pudgy, but underneath that carpet of fur, sloths are quite skinny!

PYGMY THREE-TOED SLOTH

Time-out for a fast fact: SLOTHS ARE GOOD SWIMMERS IN PART BECAUSE THEY'RE GASSY! SLOW DIGESTION MEANS THEY HAVE LOTS OF GAS IN THEIR SYSTEM, WHICH HELPS THEM FLOAT.

21

Best Smile

Say, "Leeeeeaves!" With that silly smirk, Sloth appears to be in permanent selfie mode. However, when Shark is getting ready for her close-up, you might get the urge to swim a few strokes backward! That toothy grin, whether she means it or not, reads a wee bit menacing!

Sloths

With that easygoing grin, it's hard not to smile back at a sloth. But you don't see sloths flashing their pearly whites, because their teeth aren't white at all! They're stained dark brown from the leaves they eat. Sloths' peglike teeth, which do all their chewing, are continuously growing and don't have any enamel to protect them from staining. Because sloths lack sharp teeth for biting into leaves, their hard lips take care of the job of tearing them off of branches. *Mm-mm*, lip-smacking good!

BROWN-THROATED SLOTH

Sharks

Get that great white to an orthodontist! It has perhaps the gnarliest, toothiest grin of all sharks. Its serrated teeth are arranged in rows—when it loses one tooth, there's a replacement lined up. Great whites can go through some 30,000 teeth in their lifetime! Sounds like there's no time for braces! Sharks do seem to have a serious side, and a few might just need to turn that frown upside down. Blue sharks, for example, one of the most widespread sharks, have a more frowny than fearsome face and big eyes that make them look distinctly worried. And nurse sharks have a wide-mouthed face rather like that of a catfish. Cruising the ocean floor searching for shellfish and shrimp, these bottom-feeders make a slurping sound when sucking up snacks!

GREAT WHITE SHARK

Best Outer Layer

It's that point in this throwdown to head to the runway for a front-row comparison of Shark and Sloth's outerwear. When it comes to their fur and skin, sloths and sharks have their own unique style—and they certainly won't get called out by the fashion police for twinning!

TIGER SHARK

Sharks

Sure, sharks are known for their chompers, but did you know they have teeth all over their skin, too? Sharks' skin is covered in "dermal denticles"—V-shaped overlapping scales covered in enamel (the same stuff that covers human teeth), which strengthens and protects their skin against injury. Their skin feels like sandpaper, and the denticles' pattern reduces turbulence and helps sharks move through the water faster. Many shark species also have countershading. That means the top of the body is darker than the underbelly. Sharks are camouflaged with dark ocean water when viewed from above, and still camouflaged with lighter surface water when viewed from below. Very fashion-forward, Shark!

Shark could win this battle by the skin of her teeth!

Sloths

You might have guessed that Sloth's fur isn't designed to be an aero-dynamic suit of armor. It's actually a water-resistant coat that many tiny critters catch a ride on! Never ones to feel the need to fit in, sloths are the only mammal whose hair grows backward: Their hair parts in the middle of their belly and grows up toward their back. Even the hair on their face points up, allowing rain to run off when sloths are hanging upside down! Green is definitely Sloth's color: Algae grow in the grooves of sloths' fur, offering a nice camouflage for forest living. Their fur also hosts moths, ticks, and beetles. And here's a fashion win: Three-toed sloths' facial coloring adds to their smirking, sleepy-eyed look.

Time-out for a fast fact: SCIENTISTS HAVE COUNTED 980 BEETLES LIVING IN THE FUR OF ONE SLOTH!

BROWN-THROATED SLOTH

Best Early Years

Sloth and Shark's early years match their personalities. Shark is the independent type from the get-go, and Sloth, well, he can be a little clingy.

Sloths

Sloths are committed to their life in the trees. So much so that mama sloths give birth to their babies while hanging from branches! Sloths' claws are made for holding on to tree limbs, not babies, so newborn sloths have to do some work from Day One, clinging to their mom's belly or back, where they'll stay for up to eight months. Once the baby is grown and ready to branch out, the young sloth will move along, adopting part of its mother's range in the forest.

26

Sharks

Different shark species can have very different upbringings from each other. About 40 percent of female sharks lay eggs in protective cases outside their body (there's one pup per case, and the shark pup pops out when it's ready to face the world), but others give birth to live pups! Those live births often happen in bays and estuaries, where seawater and freshwater meet, where the pups are more protected. Right after the pups are born, they're on their own, but the young'uns stick together for weeks, sometimes even years, to stay safe from predators. A shark's gotta have her squad, right?

Time-out for a fast fact: SHARKS' EGG CASES ARE CALLED MERMAID'S PURSES!

LEMON SHARK PUPS

Cutest Baby

Well hello, folks! This matchup is really heating up. Sloth and Shark just keep one-upping each other with their wow factor!

You've got that right, Peggy. This seems like a good time to hit pause and turn things over to our special correspondent, Frank. He's going to take us back to the simpler days, when Sloth and Shark were just wee little bitty ones.

Thanks, Bob! No surprise here. Our two contestants had very different upbringings! Let's start with Sloth. When he was born, he weighed less than a can of soda.

That's just adorbs!

Just wait till you hear this: Sloth babies are intense cuddlers. They cling 24/7 to Mom, who not only keeps them fed, but warm, too.

A permanent sloth hug. I want one!

Contain yourself, Bob, it's about to get cuter. Orphaned sloth babies that live at rescue sanctuaries are given stuffed animals to cling to, so they feel cozy, like they're hugging their mom.

Well that just makes me feel all warm and fuzzy.

I'm with you, Bob! Now, while sloths are major cuddle bugs, sharks are just jaw-droppingly cool!

HOFFMAN'S TWO-TOED SLOTH

Hit me with the cool stuff, Frank.

Here goes: Some sharks, like horn sharks, are born from spiral-shaped egg cases that look like a drill bit. Mama shark wedges them into nooks and crannies so predators have a hard time stealing them.

HORN SHARK

 Whoa! Hippest high-tech mom ever!

Get ready to go from the cool to the creepy. When sand tiger sharks are still in their mother's womb, they, well, eat their brothers and sisters.

WHAT?! Ack!

Yep, it's true. It's survival of the fittest, and generally only two ultimately survive.

I guess it's a shark-eat-shark world!

Oh, Bob.

 I couldn't resist!

 Whoa, I'm still recovering from the shark backstory, Frank, but we have more battles to duke out. Back to it!

Most Famous Celeb

With all of their pop culture success, both sloths and sharks are Hollywood Walk of Fame-worthy. Let's see which star has shined brighter.

Sharks

Sharks have often played the bad guy on the silver screen, starting most famously with *Jaws*, a movie (based on a book) about a gigantic great white lurking in the waters off of New England, U.S.A. Then there was the great white who chomped after Ariel and Flounder through a shipwreck in *The Little Mermaid*. And although Bruce, the great white from *Finding Nemo*, appears to be a villain, flashing his menacing grin at the movie's heroes, Dory and Marlin, we eventually learn that he and his sidekicks, a hammerhead and a shortfin mako, are vegetarians, vowing "fish are friends, not food."

Poor shark—always the villain, never the hero!

GREAT WHITE SHARK

Time-out for a fast fact:
A PHOTOGRAPHER IN FLORIDA, U.S.A., TOOK A PICTURE OF A LEMON SHARK WITH A GRIN THAT MATCHES BRUCE'S IN *FINDING NEMO*.

Ref, can I get a replay of that in slo-mo?

Sloths

Like sharks, sloths have fallen into their obvious stereotype on-screen and are forever teased for being slow. In the movie *Zootopia*, the workers at the Department of Motor Vehicles counters are all slooooooooow-moving sloths—who enjoy taking a break for a joke. In *The Croods*, Belt, a three-toed sloth, clings to a human's waist to keep the human's pants up (thus the name "Belt"). Sid, from the *Ice Age* movies, is technically a ground sloth, although not as big as ground sloths were in their day. A real sloth, named Shirley, was assistant referee at the 2018 Puppy Bowl, a Super Bowl half-time football game involving, well, puppies! Wearing a signature black-and-white-striped shirt, Shirley made calls while hanging upside down from a goalpost.

BROWN-THROATED SLOTH

Most Camera-Ready

Let's see which contender the camera loves most! Get ready for your close-up, Sloth and Shark!

BROWN-THROATED SLOTH

#flowerpower
GROOVY HIBISCUS!

MANED SLOTH

#WokeUpLikeThis
BAD HAIR. DON'T CARE!

#feelingcute
HAVING A CHILL DAY.

HOFFMAN'S
TWO-TOED SLOTH

PORT JACKSON SHARK

#puckerup
SEALED WITH A FISH.

BLUNTNOSE SEVENGILL
SHARK

#daydreaming
WEEKEND VIBE.

SCALLOPED HAMMERHEAD
SHARK

#mygoodside
KEEP OR DELETE?

TASSELLED WOBBEGONG
SHARK

#fashionable
OUTFIT OF THE DAY.

Biggest Pooper

Everyone poops, including sharks and sloths. All right, the topic of this battle is a little gross—and embarrassing—but believe it or not, you can learn a lot about an animal by their feces (the proper name for poop). Don't be so quick to flush this battle down the drain!

Sharks

When a great white shark poops, other fish come swimming. A crew of underwater photographers recently captured a great white pooping a large yellow plume, and as if the dinner bell had just rung, a swarm of smaller fish swooped in. Top predators' poop contains enough nutrients for smaller fish down the food chain to take full advantage. Scientists study shark poop to discover what the animals are eating and how much they are digesting their food. Studying fossilized shark poop has helped researchers understand what prehistoric sharks ate millions of years ago.

GREAT WHITE SHARK

Sloths

Pooping is a major event for sloths. They digest their food very slowly (no surprise here) and poop about every six days. And it's a BIG DEAL. Their pooping day is one of the only times a sloth leaves the tree canopy. Making their way to the forest floor, often to the base of the same tree, sloths do what one biologist called a "poo dance," which creates a small hole for them to poop in. When they're done, sloths head straight back up the tree. When they're away from the safety of their perch, sloths are at risk from predators. So why do they put themselves in danger and poop at ground level? It's still a mystery. Some researchers think it may give the sloths a chance to cross paths with other sloths during their otherwise solitary lives.

Time-out for
a fast fact:
A SLOTH'S POOP
CAN BE AS MUCH
AS A THIRD OF
THEIR TOTAL BODY
WEIGHT!

HOFFMAN'S TWO-TOED
SLOTH

Most Likely to Win a Staring Contest

This competition has sure been eye-opening. Speaking of peepers, both Sloth and Shark better keep an eye on their rival: They won't be able to blink during this battle, or they might just lose the title of best vision!

Sloths

Everything Sloth needs is right in front of him—and by everything, we mean leaves. Sloths rely on senses other than vision (mostly their sense of touch) to get their food because their eyesight is pretty poor. As we know, sloths don't do anything fast, and that includes blinking! They blink frequently, but very slowly—sometimes one eye at a time!

Sloth, do you have your eye on the prize? Wink, wink.

BROWN-THROATED SLOTH

Sharks

Sharks have superhero-level senses, and eyesight is one of them. Their eyes are structurally similar to humans' eyes, but they can see in dark, murky water up to 10 times better than we can. Sharks' eyes are even built for battle: Some sharks have a special membrane that protects their eyes, and great white sharks can roll their eyes back to protect themselves during an attack. But some deep-sea sharks, like bigeye threshers, have to keep their softball-size eyes open. After all, you've got to keep your eyes peeled to hunt where it's dark!

BIGEYE THRESHER SHARK

Scariest Nemesis

Sloths appear to live a happy-go-lucky lifestyle, but dangers lurk in the forest. As for sharks, sometimes they are the hunters, and sometimes they are the hunted! Sounds like Sloth and Shark better watch their back during this battle!

Top predators like great whites, tiger sharks, and hammerheads rule the seas and send their prey swimming for safety. But even these big fish have a natural ocean predator to watch out for. It's not a shark, but it has enough teeth to attack one. It's an orca, a member of the dolphin family, and it has one weapon that sharks don't: a pod. Orcas hunt as a group and have been known to attack shortfin makos and even great whites!

Sloths aren't attention-seekers; they just like to blend in. This is a major benefit when it comes to avoiding predators. Sloths have to rely on camouflage in the form of their algae-covered coats to avoid the attention of predators like jaguars, ocelots (a type of wild cat), and eagles, who are no friends to sloths. If they ever meet face-to-face, sloths will bite and hiss, and if they have to, they'll bring out their secret weapon: hooked claws! A sloth turns from cuddly cutie to serious slasher with just one swipe!

Ultimate Survivor

Sloths are naturally decked out in camo. Sharks' skin is armored for defense. Both are superb traits to have in a battle for survival. But sloths and sharks face dangers that go beyond being someone's dinner—and they aren't threats that either can protect themselves from.

Sloths

Just as sometimes you can't see the forest for the trees, you certainly can't see a sloth without a forest. Sloths are entirely dependent on tropical rainforests as their home. This is where their shelter and their food are—nowhere else. The problem is that rainforests are decreasing due to logging and the clearing of land for plantations and raising cattle. Humans are also expanding towns into rainforests. Another threat to sloths: cars. Sometimes sloths have to leave their trees to find another home, and if they have to cross a road, there's no slow lane slow enough for sloths. In Central and South America, sloth sanctuaries rescue injured and orphaned sloths and release them when they are ready to strike out on their own again.

BROWN-THROATED SLOTH

Sharks

Humans around the globe fear sharks. But in reality, you have a higher chance of getting struck by lightning than being killed by a shark. Humans are more harmful to sharks than sharks are to us. Some 100 million sharks are killed every year by "finning"—cutting off a shark's fin to make shark fin soup, a traditional Asian delicacy. Even though sharks have thrived for hundreds of millions of years, finning, along with other concerns like ocean pollution, means a quarter of all sharks are threatened with extinction.

Find out more about what you can do to help protect sloths and sharks on pages 56–57.

Weirdest Quirk

Our fierce competitors have already proven that they have some pretty unusual traits, but to take the lead in this battle, they're going to have to take it to the next level. Time to really let loose, Sloth and Shark!

Sloths

Almost all mammals—from mice to humans to giraffes—have seven vertebrae (a type of bone) in their necks. Not sloths. Two-toed sloths have either six or seven, and three-toed sloths have eight or nine! For three-toed sloths, those extra bones are what give them the ability to turn their head 270 degrees—three-quarters of the way around! (For comparison, you can turn your head about 90 degrees.) That's a pretty cool party trick, but it also lets Sloth keep an eye out for potential predators without much effort!

BROWN-THROATED SLOTH

Sharks

Here's one sure way to catch someone's eye: glow green! Swell sharks are covered in spots that appear beige in normal white light (like daylight above the water) but turn bright green when activated by underwater blue light, a process called biofluorescence. Humans can't see this swell shark light show unless they use special cameras with filters, but there's no high-tech gear necessary for the sharks. They use this display as a form of communication—to attract and recognize each other.

Time-out for a fast fact: WHEN THREATENED, A SWELL SHARK BENDS ITS BODY INTO A U-SHAPE AND SWALLOWS WATER, CAUSING IT TO SWELL TO TWICE ITS NORMAL SIZE.

It's hard not to be green with envy with a trick like that!

Wackiest Profile Pics

These photos are guaranteed to get plenty of likes!

#getoutside
GETTING MY GREENS!

HOFFMAN'S TWO-TOED SLOTH

BROWN-THROATED SLOTH

#sunsouttonguesout
MMM ... TASTY.

#gymselfie
LOOK! NO HANDS!

HOFFMAN'S
TWO-TOED SLOTH

LONGNOSE SAWSHARK

#nosy
I NOSE THIS WILL
GET A LOT OF LIKES!

#photobomb
FEELING CHUMMY.

#bffs
TOTAL BOTTOM-FEEDERS.

BASKING SHARK

#hangry
I SHOULD TRY A NEW FILTER.

NURSE SHARK

GREAT HAMMERHEAD SHARK

45

Best Sleeping Habits

All this battling is exhausting! Surely Shark and Sloth are ready to catch a few z's. Sloths have a reputation for being super snoozers, but if there's one thing we've learned about Sloth so far in this competition, he isn't all that he appears to be. And as for Shark, well, let's just say she has a surprising snuggly side.

Sharks

People used to think that sharks never slept, assuming that if they stopped moving, they'd drown. (When sharks swim, oxygen-rich water flows through their gills, which is how most sharks breathe.) Some sharks, like great whites, hammerheads, and megamouths, do enter restful states—but they don't exactly sleep the way humans do, and they still swim slowly. Other sharks, like nurse sharks, have small holes, called spiracles, near their eyes that push water across their gills. This allows them to become immobile, so much so that during the day, these nocturnal sharks flop on the seafloor to rest in a big cuddle pile!

Is Sloth really a lazybones who just snoozes the day away?

Time out to review the facts! Sloths sleep about the same amount as you do—maybe less! In the wild, sloths snooze about eight or nine hours a day. The myth that they're constantly dozing comes from the fact that they move really slowly, and people just assume they're sleeping. But that's the point: Sloths don't want to be noticed by predators; being still is the perfect disguise. Two-toed sloths generally rest in the fork of a tree, where they might look like a termite nest. Three-toed sloths hang with all four limbs together and their head tucked to their chest, so they look a bit like a clump of leaves.

HOFFMAN'S TWO-TOED SLOTH

Biggest Scientific Wonder

Can we hit pause for just one moment and agree that both sloths and sharks are among the most unique animals on the planet? Scientists have certainly taken notice: They've copied some of sharks' coolest features to improve human-made products. And believe it or not, sloths' matted green fur may hold the key to curing human diseases. Okay, Super Sloth and Super Shark, it's time to see which of you is the biggest scientific wonder!

HOFFMAN'S TWO-TOED SLOTH

Sloths

We know that sloths' fur is ... how do we put this delicately? ... buggy. Their coat hosts a whole micro-ecosystem, which, it turns out, could be very useful to scientists. Chemicals released by tiny organisms living in sloths' fur have qualities that could help cure malaria (a disease spread by mosquitoes that affects humans) or even help create new kinds of antibiotics. Put a white coat on him and call him Dr. Sloth!

You certainly have to have thick skin to get through this battle!

GREAT WHITE SHARK

Sharks

If you want to swim fast like a shark, you have to dress the part. One swimsuit company tried to create a material that was designed to mimic the sandpaper quality of sharks' skin to cut down on drag, but they couldn't replicate the complex structure that is millions of years in the making. Even the United States Navy mimics sharks: Sharks don't get barnacle and algae buildup on their skin the way other marine animals, like whales, do. On Navy ships, to prevent that buildup, which slows them down and increases fuel costs, scientists created a product to coat on the hulls that mimics the structure of sharks' skin.

Time-out for a fast fact: GREAT WHITES HAVE A SUPER SENSE OF SMELL: THEY CAN DETECT ONE DROP OF BLOOD IN 10 BILLION DROPS OF WATER!

49

Coolest
Close Encounter

As we begin to wind up this contest, it's only fitting to find out which of our two contenders would be the most fun to hang out with one-on-one. Ready for an epic sleepover? There are places where you can spend the night among sharks or hang out with sloths!

Sharks

No need to pack a wet suit for this slumber party.
Several aquariums around the world, including some in the United States and the United Kingdom, offer special events for families to spend the night next to fish tanks—including the ones with sharks! At SEA LIFE London Aquarium, kids and their parents get a special after-hours tour of the museum, play games, and then sleep in front of giant tanks with sharks of all sizes swimming about. Sweet dreams!

BROWN-THROATED SLOTH

Sloths

Now here's something dreamy: Visitors to Toucan Rescue Ranch in Costa Rica can get up close to rescued baby sloths who are learning how to climb—not on tree branches, but on rocking chairs! The number one thing baby sloths must learn is how to climb a tree, but trees in the forest don't stand still—they sway. At the rescue ranch, sloths climb on the chairs, which rock as they move around. Sloths at the ranch—which also treats and releases birds like toucans and macaws—climb and cling to the sides of rocking chairs to get the hang of life in the wild.

51

Coolest Special Feature

All right Sloth and Shark, this is your last chance to show us what you've got. If there's a supercool trick up your sleeve, now's the time to reveal it!

Sloths

Sloths snooze 100 feet (30 m) high above the forest floor, clinging to branches and never losing their grip. How do they do it? Their claws work the opposite way that your hands do: They are naturally in a closed grip. It actually takes sloths effort to open their claws. This secret weapon means sloths never have to fear going for a tumble in the middle of a nap! Okay, that's a cool tool to have in your belt, but there's more: Sloths' "claws" aren't long, hard fingernails like the claws of many other species—they're actually elongated finger bones! Kinda awesome, kinda *eww!*

Time-out for a fast fact: SLOTHS USE THEIR CLAWS—NOT THEIR MOUTH—TO CLEAN THEIR FUR.

BROWN-THROATED SLOTH

Sharks

You know how Spider-Man has a "spidey sense" that allows him to sense danger? Well, sharks have a "sharky sense," but instead of sensing trouble, they sense where to find lunch! Underneath a shark's skin, from the snout and down the sides of its body, is what's called a lateral line. The line is actually a series of canals filled with fluid and lined with hairlike cells, which sense vibration and movement and send messages to the shark's brain. When prey is moving nearby, a shark can sense it, right under its skin.

lateral line

Time-out for a fast fact:
SCIENTISTS THINK SHARKS ALSO HAVE A "COMPASS SENSE"—AN ABILITY TO NAVIGATE THE GLOBE BY SENSING CHANGES IN THEIR OWN ELECTRIC FIELD IN RELATION TO EARTH'S MAGNETIC FIELD.

Decision Time

Phew! That competition was epic!

It sure was, Peggy. I solemnly swear I will never again call a sloth lazy. I only wish I could swim like a sloth.

Seriously! And how about those sharks—glowing in the dark and sleeping in a pile? Who knew?

Not me! And you know what's next ... it's time to choose our winner!

Okay kid, it's in your hands now. Who have you chosen? Would it help to have a quick recap?

Shark Replay

Length: Up to 55 feet (17 m)
Weight: 20 tons (18 t)
Number of species: More than 400
Range: Every ocean on Earth
Cruising speed: Up to 35 miles an hour (56 km/h)
Favorite foods: Fish, krill
Sleep: Zero hours
(but some species do enter "restful states")
Greatest natural enemy: Orcas
Famous for: Jagged triangular teeth

Sloth Replay

Length: 2 feet (0.6 m)
Weight: About 17 pounds (7.7 kg)
Number of species: 6
Range: Central and South America
Cruising speed: 6 to 8 feet (1.8 to 2.4 m) a minute
Favorite food: Leaves
Sleep: 8 to 9 hours a day (in the wild)
Greatest natural enemy: Jaguars
Famous for: Hanging upside down

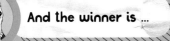
And the winner is ...

Drumroll ...

(dramatic pause)

Yay! You chose well! Nice job!

You're one smart cookie. But we're not done yet. Now that you are a sloth and shark expert, it's time to go spread your knowledge to your family and friends! Fill them in on everything you learned and then ask them: Are you on Team Sloth or Team Shark? Ask your parents to go online with you to the National Geographic Kids website, natgeokids.com/sharks-vs-sloths, where a poll is happening as we speak. Pick your preference and find out which of these cool creatures is ahead!

SHARKS VS. SLOTHS

All Together for Conservation

Sloth and Shark, you two may be complete opposites, but you both brought your A game to this battle. But even superstars need help. Sloths and sharks both face serious threats. How about we call a truce and work together to protect these amazing animals?

Sharks

Protecting sharks means protecting oceans. Tiny pieces of plastic, called microplastics, pollute the oceans' waters and are eaten by sharks and other ocean animals, exposing them to toxic chemicals. Microplastics can also damage digestive systems. How can you help? Reduce your use of plastic, recycle, and participate in a beach or river cleanup.

You can make a difference based on the type of fish you eat! For starters, shark fin soup usually has—you guessed it—shark fin in it. You know from our "Ultimate Survivor" battle how harmful finning is to the world's shark populations. Something as simple as passing up the shark fin soup on the menu saves sharks. Ask your parents to buy "sustainable seafood"— that means fish that are caught or farmed using equipment that doesn't harm other sea animals, like sharks and dolphins. The Monterey Bay Aquarium's Seafood Watch website, seafoodwatch.org, helps you choose the type of seafood to eat that is healthiest for the ocean.

Protecting sloths means protecting tropical rainforests. Rainforests once covered 14 percent of the land on Earth, but now cover only about 6 percent. Rainforest trees are logged and then milled for timber and paper. (They are also cleared for farming and building houses.) You can help by reducing your paper consumption: Reuse paper as scrap paper, and don't forget to recycle paper when it can't be used anymore—and that goes for cardboard, too!

Rainforests around the world are cleared for farmers to grow food like bananas, coffee, and palm oil. Ask your parents to look for labels on these foods that show they were grown and produced in a rainforest-friendly way.

Pygmy three-toed sloths are the most endangered of all sloth species: They are only found on one Caribbean island. Even though no one lives there permanently, growing tourism is degrading the mangrove forest that these sloths call home. One of the best ways to help wild animals is to leave them undisturbed in their habitat.

And even though they are about the cuddliest creatures you've ever seen, sloths should never be kept as pets.

QUIZ:
Are You a Sloth or a Shark?

The hard work of choosing a winner is done. Hurray! But there's one last thing we must do, which is to find out: Are YOU a sloth or a shark? Take this quiz to see if you belong in the sea or in the trees.

1 **Which best describes your fashion sense?**
A. I like to make a statement: I don't mind wearing a little color.
B. Simple: I stick with just a few basic colors.

2 **Bell rang! It's recess. You ...**
A. head for the swings.
B. join a game of tag.

3 **It's the first day of summer vacation. You ...**
A. sleep in! You waited all year for this.
B. get up with the sun. Why miss a minute of fun?

4 **Which activity would you rather do?**
A. Zip-line through a tree canopy.
B. Explore an underwater shipwreck.

5 **What do you pack in your lunch box?**
A. Pretty much the same thing every day. I'm not big on change!
B. Whatever I can find. I'll pretty much eat anything!

6 **A perfect day would be ...**
A. curling up in a hammock with a book.
B. hitting the pool and having a belly flop competition with friends.

7 **Your mom gets ready to snap your photo. You ...**
A. flash a big grin.
B. roll your eyes.

8 **You're feeling adventurous, so you ...**
A. go hang gliding.
B. go bodysurfing in the ocean.

If you answered mostly A, you officially get to hang your hat on Team Sloth! If you answered mostly B, splash on over to Team Shark!

58

Next Up:
Explore More Sloths and Sharks!

Not ready for all this sloth and shark fun to come to an end? There are other fish in the sea: Ask a grown-up to help you check out these resources to keep exploring and learn how you can help sloths and sharks!

WEBSITES

National Geographic Kids: Great White Shark
natgeokids.com/animals/great-white-shark

National Geographic Kids: Sand Tiger Shark
natgeokids.com/animals/sand-tiger-shark

National Geographic Kids: Hammerhead Shark
natgeokids.com/animals/hammerhead-shark

National Geographic Kids: Bull Shark
natgeokids.com/animals/bull-shark

Defenders of Wildlife: Basic Facts About Sharks
defenders.org/sharks/basic-facts

World Wildlife Fund: Shark
worldwildlife.org/species/shark

National Geographic Kids: Sloth
natgeokids.com/animals/sloth

World Wildlife Fund: Sloth
worldwildlife.org/species/sloth

BOOKS

Gregory, Josh. *Sloths*. Scholastic, 2015.

Mission: Shark Rescue. National Geographic Kids Books, 2016.

Musgrave, Ruth. *Everything Sharks*. National Geographic Kids Books, 2011.

Schreiber, Anne. *Sharks*. National Geographic Kids Books, 2008.

Trull, Sam. *Slothlove*. Inkshares, 2016.

Ultimate Book of Sharks. National Geographic Kids Books, 2018.

VIDEOS

A Sloth Named Velcro. PBS, 2015.

National Geographic Kids. YouTube Playlist: Shark Videos
natgeokids.com/SharkVideos

National Geographic Kids: World Oceans Day
natgeokids.com/explore/nature/world-oceans-day

HELP PROTECT SLOTHS AND SHARKS

Kids Saving the Rainforest
kidssavingtherainforest.org

Adopt a Three-Toed Sloth
gifts.worldwildlife.org/gift-center/gifts/Species-Adoptions/Three-toed-Sloth

Adopt a Great White Shark
gifts.worldwildlife.org/gift-center/gifts/Species-Adoptions/Great-White-Shark

Index

Photo Credits

HOFFMAN'S TWO-TOED SLOTH

Thanks for hanging around!

For Amy Little, whose devotion to keeping our waters clean definitely puts her on Team Shark. —JB

Since 1888, the National Geographic Society has funded more than 12,000 research, exploration, and preservation projects around the world. The Society receives funds from National Geographic Partners, LLC, funded in part by your purchase. A portion of the proceeds from this book supports this vital work. To learn more, visit natgeo.com/info.

For more information, visit nationalgeographic.com, call 1-800-647-5463, or write to the following address:

National Geographic Partners
1145 17th Street N.W.
Washington, D.C. 20036-4688 U.S.A.

Visit us online at nationalgeographic.com/books

For librarians and teachers: ngchildrensbooks.org

More for kids from National Geographic: natgeokids.com

National Geographic Kids magazine inspires children to explore their world with fun yet educational articles on animals, science, nature, and more. Using fresh storytelling and amazing photography, *Nat Geo Kids* shows kids ages 6 to 14 the fascinating truth about the world—and why they should care.
kids.nationalgeographic.com/subscribe

For information about special discounts for bulk purchases, please contact National Geographic Books Special Sales: specialsales@natgeo.com

For rights or permissions inquiries, please contact National Geographic Books Subsidiary Rights: bookrights@natgeo.com

Designed by Kathryn Robbins
Illustrations by Michael Byers

Library of Congress Cataloging-in-Publication Data

Names: Beer, Julie, author. | National Geographic Kids (Firm), publisher. | National Geographic Society (U.S.)
Title: Sharks vs. sloths / by Julie Beer.
Other titles: Sharks versus sloths
Description: Washington, DC : National Geographic Kids, [2019] | Audience: Age 8-12. | Audience: Grade 4 to 6.
Identifiers: LCCN 2018035851| ISBN 9781426335235 (hardcover) | ISBN 9781426335242 (hardcover)
Subjects: LCSH: Sharks--Juvenile literature. | Sloths--Juvenile literature.
Classification: LCC QL638.9 .B44 2019 | DDC 597.3--dc23
LC record available at https://lccn.loc.gov/2018035851

The publisher wishes to acknowledge everyone who helped make this book possible: Ariane Szu-Tu, editor; Hilary Andrews, photo editor; Molly Reid, production editor; Gus Tello and Anne LeongSon, design production assistants; and Becky Baines, for her creative input.

Printed in China
19/RRDH/1

GREAT WHITE SHARK